SCRAP

On Louise Nevelson

Julie Gard

The writing of this work was made possible in part by the voters of Minnesota through a grant from the Arrowhead Regional Arts Council, thanks to appropriations from the McKnight Foundation and the Minnesota State Legislature's general and arts and cultural heritage fund.

FIRST EDITION

copyright©2018 Julie Gard
Cover art: Michelle Matthees, *Gesture of Nevelson*, 2017
Cover design: Julie Gard

ISBN 978-0-9995921-1-3
LCCN: 2018937629

Published by Ravenna Press
(ravennapress.com)

for Michelle

Table of Contents

Foreword

I.

Self-Portrait, c. 1940 3
Exotic Landscape, 1942-45 4
Ancient City, 1945 5
Splintered Corners 6
Louise Nevelson in the Kitchen, c. 1954 7
Mike Nevelson in Egypt During the War, 1942 8
Witching Hour 9
First Personage, 1956 10
Personale I 11
Night-Focus-Dawn, 1969 12
Sky City I, 1957 13
Pair 14
Three Night Figures, 1960 15
Black Box (Seeing Through), c. 1950 16

II.
Fitting 19

Fabrication	20
Nightsphere-Light, 1969	22
323 East 30th Street	23
Transparency	24
Shadows and Flags, 1978	25
Probably without a Jacket	26
23 Spring Street	27
Personale II	28
Day Grid	29
Chapel of the Good Shepherd, 1977	30
Placements	31
Self-Defined	32

III.

Mother and Child, 1947	35
Mrs. N's Palace, 1964-77	36
Self-Portrait, Silent Music IV, 1964	37
Dawn Tree, 1976	38
Cascade, 1964	39
Grandchild	40
Black Moon, 1959	41
Sky Cathedral Presence, 1964	42
Night Leaf, 1969-1974	43

Endnote 44
The Vertical Cloud I, 1977 45
Mirror-Shadow VII, 1988 46

Notes
Acknowledgments
About the Author

Foreword

The sculptor Louise Nevelson was born in 1899 in Ukraine, grew up in Maine, and lived in New York City for most of her life. She worked with found wooden objects painted monochromatically, most often black, and also with paper, cloth and metal. Forty-two at the time of her first solo exhibit, Nevelson went on to become one of the most important American artists of the 20th century. She was also a mother.

SCRAP

On Louise Nevelson

I.

*When you square the circle,
you are in the place of wisdom.*

- Louise Nevelson

*I wasn't dumping them
on the doorstep somewhere.*

- Doris Lessing

Self-Portrait, c. 1940

to her son

Do not enter the kitchen where your mother appears to be cooking but stirs a potion, adding rust and grass and horns. She coats all of her work with it. You will do this too someday.

She gives you a hug before they take you away, one circle around you and a square in your face: her first no. Your gaze breaks against it.

Exotic Landscape, 1942-45

In this writer's midwestern house, toolbox equals green tackle box and a mess of nails and screws, drywall supports and bent metal left over from shade installations, a Phillips *and* a flathead on a good day, and clay-cutting wire. Tape measure, odd button and tack, stubborn pen, electrical tape, and one perpetually turning antique doorknob.

L.N.'s toolbox held what she needed to become what she already was: a hammer, a nail, and found wood.

Ancient City, 1945

Two winged griffins are the red sentinels at the edge of understanding. She found these creatures already made, their faces locked into grimaces, curling tongues and vital death masks, and she turned their backs to the sun. She put them on a pedestal.

What lover of representation created these accurate animals? I put a doll in my story, but who painted her hazel eyes? The person in the poem: Who raised him as a child?

This sculpture's sun is a burnt-out O and I want to know who carved it, if the artist drank when lonely.

Splintered Corners

During World War II, sculptors could not get steel. It was heavy and hard to work with, and L.N. did not like heat and noise. Besides, she had no money.

I'm not going to wait till the war is over.

You had to be famous to work big; you had to be a man. Scrap wood was light, unwanted. No one noticed two women, one clutching a bowling pin and the other a banister, hurrying down 61st Street in the rain.

Louise Nevelson in the Kitchen, c. 1954, with column from First Personage, completed 1956

She impaled herself willingly each time she worked. More nails went through the central board of her form than through Christ. The art got the light, the door, the frame, while her body stood to the side.

Her house leaked light and air. Dark realizations marched up brick steps, shuttling forth from Mrs. N's simple kitchen. This piece of her armed for battle, eased by workmen over the grate.

Mike Nevelson in Egypt During the War, 1942

He looked inward into darkness: you could say this about many. They confessed that they were dying: Louise, Doris, Paul, Charlotte, Sherwood, Joni. They sent back what they could. In Russia during the wars, mothers brought their children to train stations and simply walked away.

That struggle blinds you.

All I say is the child's survival did not come first.

I do not know if the woman in Vladivostok who gave birth to my child was an artist, but my daughter sees in the dark, lines her eyes with it in the morning. All she makes contains the end and its core of light.

Witching Hour

She tied a scarf over her hair and went out with Diana at dusk. D. drove and L.N. told her when to stop: for an old wooden wheel at the end of an alley, tennis rackets from abandoned Park Avenue lessons, a split window frame pulled out of a house.

They discovered whole stacks of waiting wood at the site of a demolition. No one wanted it, or her; this was her genius as the unnecessary artist. She could always find the wood waiting, abandoned life to darken and resurrect.

First Personage, 1956

A knot in the wood like a round scar on flesh, a place of entry, a head. I see through this portal and imagine becoming myself.

The question-curve of the front of her body, its nipple the one place she gave sustenance. Her eye, her mind, grown out of a scar.

One side of her shook the President's hand while the barbs on the other kept family at bay, scared away demands, said fuck off.

I express my admiration and she shares her wooden answer, her measured half-embrace.

Personale I

My daughter calls while I am writing; she needs her swimsuit at school. L.N. would not have heard the phone, she would have let it ring, the gray cat wait out in the sun. She worked with scraps of wood, not time or mind.

I answer the phone and open the door, then return to the half-blank page. There is a swimsuit written on it and a daughter, and a cat hair in my tea which is now in my throat. That's how hard it is to continue working.

Night-Focus-Dawn, 1969

L.N. left behind masses of wood fiber and paint, all the water, soil and sun that growing trees turned into solid presence. The cells of her work are strong, thick houses of memory, her afterlife's sharp mind.

These parts remain in synagogues, skyscrapers, parks, museums and basements. Some are ash, like the canvases she burned in 1945 when WPA was over.

Paint my sculptures every ten years —

but no one does and nature, which she never much liked, consumes them.

Sky City I, 1957

The chair meets a dumbbell, the spool a chair, while oak oars row toward no association.

Flowerpots filled with shadows hold up walls of baseboard and a carved mouse lair with ship's portals for eyes, while one boomerang fails to return. Stitches of nail in the scrap of a seed have nothing to do with a giant spool, and banisters meticulously created by another artist's hand form tension with Hudson River drift.

In a long box with a paddle, my tall daughter dreams of kayaks while I chew at a nail in the crate next door, the wall between us thinking only of itself.

Pair

L.N. told her son twice, he said to the press, that she wished he had never been born.

His sculptures are warm and human. They hold and give the shade of trees. They form faces and shoulders and ask to be touched; they listen to the wood.

Three Night Figures, 1960

I reach out for the fiddlehead fern and word from a cave, which she holds before me in a dry blue palm. Each anchor has its shaft, its weight, its curve in her latest story. Each holds sleep.

I admire˙ her willow self, its bending, bowing strictness. She makes the rules and clips them into scraps.

Three sleep in this house, at least for now. This is her only gift.

Black Box (Seeing Through), c. 1950

In the owl's eye is his voice. He watches every scratched surface. His precarious balance is night's last dream, the coffin quiet of woods before small birds start singing. On the other side of the owl's eye waits morning. Around him, dark shapes cluster into trees. Within him, a tar-pitched road divides the forest from itself.

II.

*Somewhere in the city of New York
there are four or five still-unknown objects...
Once together they'll make a work of art.*

- Charles Simic on Joseph Cornell

*Now people might say, oh, aren't you selfish?
Well, I don't know what they mean.*

- Louise Nevelson

Fitting

My daughter and I take two small planes out East. There is much repacking of bags so that compartment doors close and backpacks fit under seats. We expose our books and underwear, stuff bathing suits into shoes. We close and open and push and pull, fit objects impossibly close.

My daughter frowns while I smile, which she finds maddening and so on, until all is stowed but our faces: two opposite masks.

Fabrication

I leave my child with her grandparents for three days - L.N. did the same on the scale of years – and on the way to New York stay with my brother and his wife.

They are artists, she is pregnant, and they have a dream of the country, a farmhouse and a barn. They talk of New Fairfield, Connecticut and a place that once belonged to L.N.'s son. I got the sense, my brother says, that he worked on her stuff more than his own.

And I tell my brother what Louise said at a party –

I've done everything alone. I don't accept help,

and Mike got so upset he almost passed out.

If no one ever helped you, I don't know what the hell I've been doing.

His daughters thought he was having a heart attack.

A mythic life is a myth, I say, but the woman made spines from chairs.

Nightsphere-Light, 1969

The wall emerges through a hairline crack in locked black theater doors, one strike, one slice of her later, more regimented, geometrical black wooden boxes. This is all I can see, as hard as I press my face.

I've come from Minnesota, and I only need a minute,

but the man in the ticket booth has no key. The Julliard admissions officer can schedule a tour in two weeks. One security guard, admitting to avid sketching, has a bit of time and a sandwich in his right hand. He opens the door with his left.

Interior blackness makes wall not wall but a hideout to visually crawl into. A plane to enter, a haunted surface that turns the side of the theater into a trap. I slide along it, known but unseen, for as long as the opening lasts.

323 East 30th Street

L.N. stayed in her first brownstone until 1958, collecting wooden debris from surrounding fallen buildings. She slept on a cot with an army blanket up to the demolition, preparing her third exhibition. She rested just enough to continue working.

Now a series of concrete cubes rises up past the treeline, square upon square of squinting white blinds and the occasional torn red curtain like an injured retina. Here and there a web of cracked window, water stains on powdered cement, and an old Ukrainian couple pushing open glass doors.

Transparency

Lemon curd leaks from a warm roll and I lick it from my wrist. I have never been willing to starve for art, live on anchovies and tea like L.N. said she could. Tea with dripping fruit and warm bread – maybe.

On the other side of café window, a tall man in dreads moves from the knees. He wears a turban with twine wrapped around it, cloth patterned with French words circling his head and rippling, as decadent as L.N. in her peasant headwraps. A rope and suspenders keep his dress pants up. Spidey t-shirt and gold chain.

He turns to fix his hair in the window and watches his reflection, female, redheaded, take a sip of green tea.

Shadows and Flags, 1978

The vision was of morning coffee on a bench in Louise Nevelson Plaza, bright sun and her name felt in each of the three sharp corners, but Shadows and Flags is a torn-up mess, shooting black points above a triangle of turned earth, cranes and orange plastic fence. So I squint out at the furl of L.N.'s black flag framed by a Budweiser sign and rotating spit of small chickens.

Even up close, the dark, planned sharpness of her sculpture does not move me, not like the dense, clumsy earth lugged and dropped by the crane, the soft people moving between hard buildings, squares and circles creating the city.

Probably without a Jacket

What I love about L.N.: the way she uses scraps, the discarded, negatives. Unused bits of wood from one project become integral to the next. What she found around the corner, what was abandoned.

Meanwhile, her son sat on the stoop during a party, locked out and found by the police. He wasn't a man who could give her anything, sex or jewelry or money or food, just a boy she had made herself.

Is it possible to create from a place of consistency, where what is lived is what is written is what is lived. Question mark.

23 Spring Street

L.N.'s second home was torn down for a gift shop and orthodontist, so I cross the street and pretend she lived in a solid, blue-doored brownstone. The gallery down the block is empty, walls flat with pop culture and harsh attempts, and I feel how art strikes or doesn't, is as visceral and irrational as love. Desire to know so strong that every breath becomes a question, and the asking stops only when life stops.

Personale II

Even during my three days alone, I am with my daughter in thoughts, worries, texts. I try to provide her with attachment, with structure, making up for the lost years. I channel the ones who stayed over the course of decades, through creative silence – Grace, Muriel, Tillie, Kathe.

The life in the child is no opposite to the life in art: they demand the same force and breath. This is the gift, the bind.

Day Grid

In lower Manhattan a black iron grate makes strict, predictable gridwork of a patch of the underground city – box of scattered receipts, wrappers and cigarettes swimming in water, spit, wet cube of air, trash and fluid flowing beneath the earth. Chaos framed by a measured, orderly system.

Chapel of the Good Shepherd, 1977

First jazz then organ, variations but always music from the sanctuary next door, and an echoing voice: *I'm doing the garbanzos with a basil dressing.*

I lay down my notebook on a wooden pew. The chapel-sculpture drenches me in white instead of black but the feeling is just as complete: a totality. Sun breaks on the altar, busts it. Faultlines of light fill the room, and I hold my breath to watch them fissure and grow.

L.N. went from recognizable objects to plywood scrap — simpler, less tooled pieces — and deliberate shapes, less haunted, but deeply intentional in their relation to each other, taken apart and put together in a historied way.

Most moving are not the fine circles but the scrap wood they were cut from, lining the walls like fragile bone. The chapel is not spirit but its diagram, belief not in the harvest but the shape of wheat.

Placements

My daughter was fine without me, though she slept in late and ate less fruit. I require that we embrace; then she is back to physically absorbing her grandparents' cable TV.

I take the hot attic room and write when not helping my mother sort fuzzed Christmas ornaments, depleted Lego sets, worn afghans – my old forts – and splintered picture frames. We choose what to keep and what to release, even the Depression glass sweating.

Self-Defined

Long after we return to the Midwest, the man whose head was wrapped with twine peers into café window. I recreate my viewpoint from inside the box, taste lemon curd, and view the city's arrangement like L. N.'s white wood in the chapel: squares and circles overlapping, a planned human chaos.

He fixes the hang of his shirt and the set of his headscarf not in the glass, but in the building's shining granite, rearranging and putting his pieces together. He is resourceful in making beauty, like a sculptor or a daughter, and I watch him break clean from the surface, shouldering everything he owns.

III.

*Look, dear, we walk on two feet. So we're
vertical. That doesn't mean the work has
to be vertical, but it means that there is
a weight within ourselves, or this flight.*

- Louise Nevelson

*O Louise. . .
You bring me to my knees*

- Ferron

Mother and Child, 1947

The museum registrar wears white cloth gloves. She is angular, spare and hopeful in her thin sweater. I can feel her life beginning and mine at its core. We talk of writing on the way down to the archives, then fall silent in front of a small, dark form on a table under light.

Body emerges from body, the child grows out of the mother, some life force at work, but the connection is strained, pose awkward, all grimace and square. The child is calmest when facing away, and both mother and child have many faces.

The registrar hands me her gloves and I feel through them, touch hollow tattistone, a flyweight mix of ash and glue. I press into each decision as L.N. molded what was left after fire, forging knowledge from what she did not know.

Mrs. N's Palace, 1964-77

In my mind I've walked within it, heard the neighbor kids call, *Mrs. N!*

Her palace is safe, wild immersion; there are mirrors and sinks and a whole world of pieces all finding places, a communion of misfits. It's a simple place to live, a grand palace, and a walk through her head. Not so different from the heart I moved through as a child in the science museum, pumping and all of its owner.

All black, this palace. Comforting and sinister in the way of the neighbor lady who, from a distance, helped to raise us.

Self-Portrait, Silent Music IV, 1964

Are divides ever this distinct? I'm not sure what they say to each other, the music note and the bird through black walls. I love this glimmer of ash, matte surface and phantom seagull whose profile senses its child through the dark scrim between them.

L.N. craved music and she played this way, in measures divided on the page but united in playing. One note, one box, leads into another. The hole at bottom right is a cavern in my own chest, the emptiness between organs, silence holding sound.

Dawn Tree, 1976

I'm alone in the middle of the city and knock a minor scale on metal branches, trace lines dropping into curves.

An imperious girl in a short bell of skirt leaps from nowhere onto the sculpture. She poses behind a pointed leaf, stares unblinking into the eye of her sister's camera.

Three six-year-olds in purple enter dawn tree like she's any other jungle, beating out bold music with their feet. They weave brightly through the dark teeth of this loom.

Cascade, 1964

Every corner in her work is one in my own mind. Just yesterday I lost that splintered box within a box. The curved shelf would be perfect for photographs, over the bed, and I'd put my wine in the bottom bin and my playing cards in that thin partitioned one. The Morse code of the centerpiece says words I've learned but lost: meet me on the other side.

I picture it just beyond the June garden and across the railroad tracks, where teenagers collect rusted tacks, nails and anvils, anything solemn and heavy. They bring the relics into the house and set them on the mantle, not into the fire but above it.

Grandchild

Her granddaughter lives in a shack with a chicken in Miami. She looks like L.N. and lives on change, with a jutting collarbone that never healed right, and she paints compulsively.

Here's the rest of your life, the moon said to her one night, and a brush to get you through it. Here's a bicycle to ride and a horse to paint. Don't lose your photograph with Salvador Dali.

She tried to catch the moon but it slid away, so for fifty years she has painted hooves and light breaking through her own skin.

Black Moon, 1959

The world's oldest television set leaks its burnt picture. Around the implosion, all life goes dark. Even the moon is held up by something. One hole stares at another and the eye turns into ash. The moon turns into an eye.

Sky Cathedral Presence, 1964

What balls this woman had, how she built up mass, compiled and added, created and opened doors, ripped them off. Innards exposed and rough, misshapen wood / splintery, loggish, ravaged. Monumental expression of annihilaton and faith, making do and more than. Exceeding, excess in perfect proportion, just right.

Gun rack and cord of wood – a bomb shelter after the bomb. Reorganized, serene, formally surviving.

Night Leaf, 1969-1974

A fan, a machine, made or found, grown or buried. Nine blades whir. A fractured engine, a loam-thick spring with nine accompanying memories. A lover's plane takes off and a fan cools the bedroom. Night claims the thick of trees. The lost one's face is this smooth, this real: white neck against black collar, white collar against black neck.

Endnote

L.N. made and transcended boundaries. These acts can happen together: embodiment of limits <u>and</u> eternity. When text is centered and squared on a page, the white space around becomes universe. Everything not word is sky. The reader grounds her eye in a block of word, or spreads with air in every direction. Straight edges verge on open white, to touch mark untouch fold.

The Vertical Cloud I, 1977

I lean over a table in the archives of the Minneapolis Institute of Art, watching a nuclear sky create its own burst in construction paper and lace. An active, changing atmosphere has been captured right before shift into quiet; L. N. caught it in otherworldly stitching, a nimble-fingered woman and persistent spider working together, joining creation and destruction at their edges.

Each superimposed detail is not a detail at all but a small separate story, told just once, so listen the first time. Observe her in old age, making bars of gold and buying the world.

Mirror-Shadow VII, 1988

L.N. put the circle outside the box so close to the end of her life. Nipple, pine cone, dowel rod all compacted into square, and then to the left, floating off: One empty, hovering round with nail holes. Quiet and tenuous seams.

A dance around the cube is its own magic sphere. She made arcs with her arms as she hammered, reached for nails, paint and stacked wood. She moved in circles like her last mirror moon, which reflects and contains every shape the way that black, to her, held every color.

The square holds up the circle, leads back to it. They are balanced, calibrated. A tired mother's vestibule, a dying artist's last visitor, the shape of her final sound. O.

Notes

Section I
Epigraphs: Louise Nevelson with Diana McKown. *Dawns and Dusks*. Charles Scribner's Sons, 1976, p. 44. / Monica Attard. "Doris Lessing: Nobel Laureate (Sunday Profile)." *Australian Broadcasting Corporation,* 21 October 2007, http://www.abc.net.au/sundayprofile/stories/s2065058.htm.

"Splintered Corners": Italics are Louise Nevelson's words, quoted from "Louise Nevelson: A Story in Sculpture." Brooke Kamin Rapaport. *The Sculpture of Louise Nevelson: Constructing a Legend.* Yale University Press, 2008, p. 10.

"Louise Nevelson in the Kitchen, c. 1954": Rapaport, p. 176 (photograph referenced).

"Mike Nevelson in Egypt During the War": *Dawns and Dusks,* p. 77 (image referenced) and p. 46 (quote).

"Night-Focus-Dawn 1969": Italics are paraphrased from Louise Nevelson's words in Harriet F. Senie's "Louise Nevelson's Public Art" in Rapaport, p. 63.

"Pair": Biographical information from "Louise Nevelson, Sacred Monster, Takes a Bow." Anita Gates. *New York Times,* 1 February 2002.

Section II
Epigraphs: Charles Simic. *Dime-Store Alchemy: The Art of Joseph Cornell.* New York Review Books, 1992, p. 14. / *Dawns and Dusks,* p. 3.

"Fabrication": Laurie Lisle. *Louise Nevelson: A Passionate Life.* Summit Books, 1990, p. 275. (Louise Nevelson's words paraphrased; Mike Nevelson's words quoted.)

"Probably without a Jacket": Biographical information from Lisle, p. 90.

Section III
Epigraph: *Dawns and Dusks,* p. 120. / Ferron. "Who Loses." *Testimony,* Lucy Records, 1980.

"Grandchild": Biographical information from Forrest Norman. "A Brush with Death." *Miami New Times,* 24 June 2004.

Acknowledgments

"Black Box (Seeing Through), c. 1950" and "Ancient City, 1945" appeared in *Ekphrasis,* Fall 2010.

All poems in Section I, along with "Self-Portrait, Silent Music IV, 1964," "Night Leaf, 1969-1974," and "Black Moon, 1959," appeared as "Saw and Scrim: On Nevelson" in *Blackbox Manifold,* October 2011.

The following poems appeared as "Shape Music: On Louise Nevelson" in *The 22 Magazine,* Spring 2014: "Fitting," "Shadows and Flags, 1978," "Probably without a Jacket," "23 Spring Street," "Personale I," "Day Grid," "Chapel of the Good Shepherd, 1977," "Placement," and "Self-Defined."

The author is grateful to staff at the Minneapolis Institute of Arts and the Walker Art Center for access to Louise Nevelson's work in their archives.

About the Author

Julie Gard is an Associate Professor of Writing at the University of Wisconsin Superior. Her prose poetry collection *Home Studies* (New Rivers Press) was a finalist for the 2016 Minnesota Book Award, and her chapbooks include *Obscura: The Daguerreotype Series* (Finishing Line Press) and *Russia in 17 Objects* (Tiger's Eye Press). Her poems, stories and essays have appeared in *Gertrude, Fourth River, Clackamas Literary Review, Crab Orchard Review, Ekphrasis* and *Blackbox Manifold,* among other journals and anthologies. A former Fulbright Graduate Fellow in Vladivostok, Russia, she lives a block from Lake Superior in Duluth, Minnesota. Her website is: www.juliegard.com